Ways to Teach Bible Reading

Easy-to-do Activities for Ages 3 -12

Publisher ....Arthur L. Miley

Author ....Nancy S. Williamson

Editor ....Crystal Abell

Art Director ....Gary Zupkas

Production Director ....Barbara Bucher

Word Processor ....Valerie Fetrow

Illustrator ....Fran Kizer

Production Artist ....Nelson Beltran

Proofreader ....Barbara Bucher

D1293885

Copyright 1991 • First Printing
Rainbow Books • P.O. Box 261129 • San Diego, CA 92196

#RB36106

But as for you, continue in what you have learned
and have become convinced of,
because you know those from whom you learned it,
and how from infancy you have known the holy Scriptures,
which are able to make you wise for salvation
through faith in Christ Jesus.
II Timothy 3:14-15 (NIV)

52 Ways to Teach Bible Reading

—**Easy-to-do Activities for Ages 3 -12**—

Introduction

The Bible is the Word of God for man — for each of us, adult or child. But if the Bible remains unopened on the table or shelf, or it is quoted incorrectly or misunderstood, its beneficial qualities are obscured. In order to allow the Bible to speak to us, we need to get it open and dig in to find the truth, to find the encouragement, challenge, comfort, compassion, strength and love that are within its pages. And as teachers of children, this should be one of our most important priorities.

Perhaps at one time the collective body of Christian educators felt it was enough for children to memorize some Bible verses, become familiar with a few Bible stories, and maybe learn how to look up different passages. Now, however, with the rapidly declining moral and spiritual condition of the world in which children are growing, we realize that children need much more. Boys and girls must have help in understanding God's Word so that they can turn to it for daily guidance and direction in their lives. Their needs and the challenges they face in today's world are so much more intense than in earlier years; in this age of torn-apart families, boys and girls need to know that there is One who cares and sticks closer to us than a brother. They need to know of God's concern for them. They need to know the goodness and power and grace of God.

Through the reading of God's Word, they *can* know these things. We must therefore adopt a more serious attitude and concentrate our efforts toward helping children learn to look to God through His written Word.

The activities in *52 Ways To Teach Bible Reading* present an experience-centered approach to the study of God's Word. They propose to help students know and to carry out in everyday living God's purposes for their lives and the lives of others. The games, puzzles, crafts, bulletin boards, guides for discussion, and so on will help the children in your classroom understand how to find guidance in the Bible. To help you choose which of the 52 ways you will utilize for your students, each activity is geared for a particular age group. (If you wish to use something for younger children who are just learning to read, you may want to provide special children's Bibles with large print and simplified words.)

52 Ways To Teach Bible Reading is intended to present Scripture not only as a record of God's dealings with people in the long ago, but also as the Word of the living God that can change lives today and lead children to accept Jesus Christ as their Savior. Keep this in mind as you use it, and it is sure to make a difference in your students' lives.

52
Ways to Teach Bible Reading
Easy-to-do Activities for Ages 3-12

CONTENTS

Unless marked otherwise, all Scripture verses are from the King James Version.

1 Lighted Paths

OBJECTIVE: To motivate children to read the Bible by holding a reading contest

Appropriate for ages 8 to 12

The best way for children to know how God is guiding their lives is for them to read His Word. Psalm 119:105 says, "Thy word is a lamp unto my feet, and a light unto my path." Use this Scripture as the basis for a contest to encourage your students to diligently and regularly read the Bible.

First, prepare a large banner to hang across the room announcing the contest: write TAKING A STEP IN THE **LIGHT** DIRECTION across the top and include the verse, as shown in the illustration. Duplicate the pattern below so that you have several dozen feet. The children will cut these out and use them as they "follow the light."

Explain to your class that in order to participate in the contest, each student must read at least two books of the Bible. (Younger children could read chapters rather than books to qualify for the contest.) When a child reads his first two books or chapters he earns a foot; he may write on it his name and the reference of the Scripture he has read. The children should be able to give a brief oral "book report" before getting a foot. Give a foot to each child for every book or chapter he reads throughout the contest.

Give each child a specific area on the classroom wall to display his feet. The students will enjoy arranging their feet in various "walking patterns" on the wall. If desired, the children may write

their book reports so that they can be displayed next to their feet. When a child has earned ten feet, write his name on a LIGHTED PATH READING AWARD scroll that you have placed somewhere in the church for everyone to see.

At the end of the quarter (or whenever you choose to end the contest), plan to give special recognition to the student who earned the most feet.

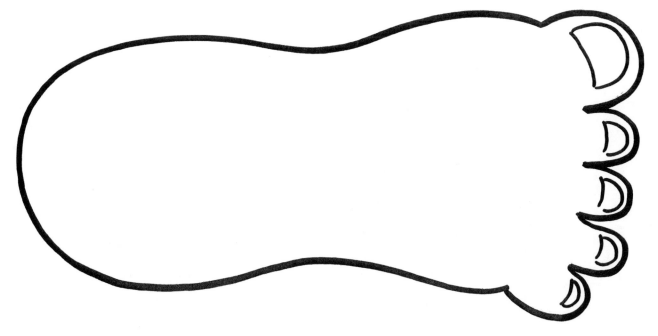

2 **Balloon Day**

OBJECTIVE: To help children get excited about regular Bible reading

Appropriate for ages 7 to 10

To help spark interest in reading the Bible, plan a "Balloon Day" as the culmination of a reading program for your class. With the help of your students, select a target date. Then invite each child to sign a contract agreeing to read a certain number of chapters or books of the Bible related to your unit of study. The contract on page 9 may be reproduced for use with this activity.

During the course of the reading program, display a poster showing the names of those who signed contracts. To keep track of progress and to promote enthusiasm, write the title for each book read on a paper balloon and tape the "marker" by the child's name when he completes the chapter or book.

On the Balloon Day, make sure you have enough helium-filled balloons for each student in your class, plus extra ones for those who fulfilled their contracts. Make this a festive party. Play games using balloons, such as Balloon Charades. Write instructions for charades and place them inside balloons. Inflate the balloons and tape them to a wall, allowing the children to burst whichever balloon they wish to and play out the charade. Another game is Balloon Bust. Each child places a balloon on his chair and at a starting signal tries to bust his balloon first. There are also many types of relay games that can be played with balloons. The children will enjoy making up their own games.

For refreshments serve colored popcorn balls with strings attached to represent balloons and a colorful fruit punch.

For a devotional let several children share their favorite Bible passages that they have read.

You may want to promote the balloon party as an all-church or Sunday school event to provide proper recognition for the participants.

READING CONTRACT

I, _____, do solemnly agree that I will read

_____ chapters or books of the Bible related to my unit of study. I further

agree that my reading will be completed by the _____ day of

_____, 19_____.

_____
(Signature)

_____   _____
(Witness/Teacher)   (Date)

---

3   Bible Belts

OBJECTIVE: To help children explain to each other what they have read in the Bible

Appropriate for ages 9 to 12

This motivational idea — awarding belts of various colors to students who meet certain goals — has worked well in public schools. Use it to help encourage your students to read the Bible.

Determine how many books of the Bible or chapters the children in your class must read to reach the different belt levels. To earn a Bible belt, a child must be able to tell the rest of the class what the chapter or book was about and any main character or event.

Create a bulletin board or poster board chart to record the students' progress. Using a progressive belt color system such as this will help stimulate a feeling of success as each child earns the next color of Bible belt (white, yellow, blue, brown, and black). When a child earns a belt, take his picture and place the photo in the proper section of the chart. Present him with a ribbon with a Bible sticker at the top. Hopefully you'll have a class full of children with black belts!

NAME	WHITE	YELLOW	BLUE	BROWN	BLACK
KEITH		☺			
BILLY			☺		
PAULA		☺			
CHRIS			☺		
KENNY				☺	
LAURA					

4 Reading Tree

OBJECTIVE: To motivate children to read the Bible using a "hands-on" activity center

Appropriate for ages 8 to 12

Save a used coffee can that will be big enough to hold a small tree branch at least a foot high. Cover the can using colorful construction paper or adhesive-backed plastic and print the words "Reading Tree" on the side. Below this print the following verse and include the reference: "The fruit of the righteous is a tree of life" (Proverbs 11:30a). If desired, you may also decorate the can with pictures that you have cut out from magazines or from leftover take-home papers or teaching aids. The pictures could illustrate various biblical concepts, such as being kind to one another, praying for salvation, listening to parents, or telling others about Jesus Christ, etc., or they could simply be colorful pictures of children in various activities. Find a tree branch to fit into the can and "plant" it by surrounding it with sand.

To help your Reading Tree come to life, make "Scripture apples" for your students to "pick" before class sessions begin or at other free times. Use the pattern on page 11 to cut out several dozen apples from red construction paper. Write a Scripture reference at the top of each apple, then write a question for the students to answer. Tie the apples on the twigs of the branch with green yarn.

This will make a good motivational interest center for your classroom. The children can pick an apple, read the question and the reference, write an answer on the back of the apple and then tie it back on the tree. Be sure to tell the students that they may write either the Scriptural answer or paraphrase it into their own words.

The following are some references and questions to help get you started:

- Psalm 144:15 — What does the Bible tell me about feeling happy? ("Happy is that people, whose God is the Lord.")
- Psalm 56:3 — Can the Bible help me when I am frightened? ("What time I am afraid, I will trust in Thee.")
- Romans 8:28 — What does the Bible say to me when I have been disappointed or hurt? ("And we know that all things work together for good to them that love God.")
- Ephesians 4:29 — What does the Bible tell me about gossiping? ("Let no corrupt communication proceed out of your mouth, but that which is good to the use of edifying, that it may minister grace unto the hearers.")
- Matthew 26:41 — Can the Bible speak to me when I am tempted to do wrong? (Jesus said, "Watch and pray, that ye enter not into temptation.")
- I John 1:9 — What does the Bible say to me when I have done wrong and feel guilty? ("If we confess our sins, He is faithful and just to forgive us our sins, and to cleanse us from all unrighteousness.")
- Romans 12:1 — What does the Bible say to me when I love God, and want to give Him my whole life? ("Present your bodies a living sacrifice, holy, acceptable unto God.")
- Philippians 4:13 — What hope does the Bible give me when I need help? ("I can do all things through Christ which strengtheneth me.")
- Matthew 5:44 — What does the Bible tell me to do when someone has been mean to me? ("I (Jesus) say unto you, 'Do good to them that hate you, and pray for them which despitefully use you.'")
- II Timothy 2:15 — What does the Bible say about how I should try to live my life? ("Study to show thyself approved unto God.")
- James 4:8 — What does the Bible say to me

when I feel lonely? ("Draw nigh to God, and He will draw nigh to you.")

- Genesis 1:31 — What did God say about all that He had created, which includes me? ("God saw every thing that He had made, and, behold, it was very good.")
- Revelation 3:20 — Does the Bible say that Jesus will come into my heart? ("Behold, I stand at the door, and knock: if any man hear My voice, and open the door, I will come in to him, and will sup with him, and he with Me.")
- 3 John 11 — What does the Bible say about the choices I should make? ("Beloved, follow not that which is evil, but that which is good.")
- James 1:22 — What does the Bible tell me I should do after I read the Scriptures? ("Be ye doers of the word, and not hearers only.")
- Ephesians 6:1-3 — What does the Bible say about my relationship with my parents? ("Children, obey your parents in the Lord: for this is right. Honor thy father and mother; which is the first commandment with promise; That it may be well with thee, and thou mayest live long on the earth.")
- Ephesians 4:32 — What does the Bible tell me about my relationship with others? ("Be ye kind one to another, tenderhearted, forgiving one another, even as God for Christ's sake

PSALM 56:3

CAN THE BIBLE HELP ME WHEN I AM FRIGHTENED?

hath forgiven you.")

- Acts 16:31 — What does the Bible say I must do to be saved? ("Believe on the Lord Jesus Christ, and thou shalt be saved, and thy house.")
- Mark 16:15 — Does the Bible say I should tell others about becoming a Christian? ("He (Jesus) said unto them, 'Go ye into all the world, and preach the gospel to every creature.'")

5 Bible Readers' Railroad

OBJECTIVE: To give positive reinforcement to students as they read God's Word

Appropriate for ages 6 to 9

Create a motivating bulletin board that doubles as a way to recognize those students who set an example of reading God's Word. Cut out a construction paper train with enough cars for all the children in your class. Make windows that are large enough to display photographs of the students. (Use an instant camera, or perhaps ask each child to supply a school photo). Using pre-cut letters or ones that you make yourself, write out the title "Bible Readers' Railroad" on the bulletin board and pin the train cars underneath.

The first child to finish five chapters or books of the Bible (you decide, based on the age level of your class) becomes the engineer. The next becomes the brakeman, and the rest will be passengers.

If desired, give more students a chance to become the engineer by "changing shifts" with each new unit of study.

6 Bible Words Puzzle

OBJECTIVE: To discover specific words that the Bible uses to describe what it offers

Appropriate for age 9 to teens

Unlike most books, the Bible speaks about itself, and rightly so. It is the God-breathed Word from heaven to earth. No other book even comes close to offering what the Bible does, for through Scripture we find encouragement, guidance, discipline, assurance, and most important, redemption.

As a way to introduce these concepts to your class, ask the children to look up the following verses. Choose a student to read a verse, then ask the class what descriptive words or names were mentioned.

Duplicate for each child the Bible Words Puzzle found on page 13 to complete after discussion time. Answers are on page 64.

Use the following Scriptures:

Psalm 119:105	Acts 17:11
Romans 15:4	II Timothy 3:15-16
Colossians 3:16	Psalm 119:140
Psalm 119:160	John 15:3

Bible Words Puzzle

Many verses in the Bible tell us what God's Word can bring to those who read it. For instance, the Bible offers peace, encouragement, and guidance. Other verses include descriptive words about the Bible, such as "sword."

The words listed below are hidden in the puzzle — across, down, backwards, and diagonally. When you find a word, draw a loop around it and cross it off the list.

COMFORT DOCTRINE FAITH LAMP
PURE SALVATION TEACHING RIGHTEOUSNESS
TRUTH INSPIRATION CORRECTION GRACE
LEARNING PATIENCE LIGHT SONGS
HOPE WISDOM READINESS

```
Q I P V B Z E X Y L I D Y S N S P S C B L H
V L U W J E M S G D G X H R S M H L O O J N
X I M W V C C I W F F U Y R O L V H R Y L N
D G J O F M F A L L Y F G D N V H T R T I J
A H L P D M K D R N Z A D U G B B J E V Z D
E T X E Z S X I S G X E L F S Y F V C Z N C
D F B N P F I H S I C B B L I A P X T N U F
N H N A F N G W N B J C L F E T B T I U B V
H E W U P O C S N L R P I Q L A L V O G O B
Z Z G G C I U S Y V M N X Q H Y R C N C K I
D K U Q Y T P E Y J E F R S F J B N L G M S
M I G G C A L N R P E N O K E B L I I E A P
B D H G O R X I V U B Z L C T B I T B N A F
I F W S Z I D D B P S B N X B K D K O S G Q
X Y Z Q X P N A Z Y Y E E O U Y J Q U X L Y
D V Z X Z S Z E Y S I H A V U W U U E D T E
G Y A T N N K R T T H E O X O T E B F W H Q
H D T A N I L I A R B I D P Q I K O L S U Y
X H G J P D T P B X L G L R E M N U O F O S
T C H D V Q C N C J S S V D O R B G T P S Y
U W E U V X Z O X O C D M G Q Z W P M A L P
X Z V W C D D Q F M R I S W E X Z N C F C G
F O E V Q A D X Q J G N B D A M R G A C X L
E U Q C Y U A C S H S K O F H D L T W F D G
C P O F A I T H B P E L D U S S Q M C C W F
L Y X D Y N K G X W E D T C O M F O R T X W
K U I E E R Y U K N N R R D Q M Y J N A K X
A I T E D D G K I R W K U R P B M N J M I Z
L D V E S P A R Z E K R T O Y R D S L B W X
Q F H I A P T I K T R R H G B V Q H B Y G J
Y G Q Y N C N M J K Z D O P D S S K G J P O
R J X G O Y H K A S S E N S U O E T H G I R
P V Z D F I T I N W Q R W P B I O E X O X T
W J U S S M X V N O R E L A E G X Z U Q C M
G E K V D W P O O G K G J Z U P C A D I V C
E R G C F I M Y H Y G D M U C E P Y U P H C
P U S V V R I P N C N O I T A V L A S G C J
J P K N L Z N I M N Z C T U S B H B I P J P
```

13

7 Bible Bookmarks

OBJECTIVE: To create a visual reminder to read the Bible daily

Appropriate for ages 8 to 10

Encourage the children in your class to read their Bibles every day by helping them to make creative bookmarks.

Duplicate the pattern below onto construction paper in a variety of colors. Let the children choose which color they want and provide scissors for them to cut out the strips.

Provide stickers for the boys and girls to put on underneath the verse and crayons or pencils to write down their names on the line.

Ahead of class time, gather scraps of material in a variety of patterns and colors. Cut the scraps into relatively small pieces so that the children will be able to readily use them. Put the assortment of fabrics in the middle of the table(s) and let the students pick out the pieces they want. They will glue the material to the back side of their bookmarks, so encourage the boys and girls to be as creative as they can. If a child wants to use one long piece that is just the shape of the rectangle, that is fine; if another wishes to glue several pieces in a mosaic fashion, that is also fine.

To help make the bookmarks more lasting, laminate or cover with clear adhesive-backed plastic.

When the class is finished with the craft, say the verse together. Ask the students to name the different books in which they could use their bookmarks, such as textbooks, library books, and of course the Bible itself. Encourage the children to look at the verse often to help them remember why we read the Bible.

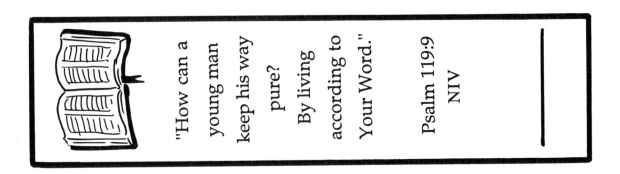

"How can a young man keep his way pure? By living according to Your Word." Psalm 119:9 NIV

8 Rebus Reading

OBJECTIVE: To enhance understanding of the Bible by visualizing its stories

Appropriate for ages 4 to 10

A rebus story is one in which pictures are substituted for words in various parts of a sentence or paragraph. Your students can create a rebus story to tell a particular Bible event or illustrate a passage of Scripture. The craft will foster a better understanding of the meaning and perhaps help the young boys and girls remember that meaning for a longer period of time.

Select a story or passage for the children to illustrate—either one that you have used recently or one that you tell just before craft time. Write out the story ahead of time on a blank sheet of 8 1/2 by 11 inch paper, leaving spaces for the pictures and including the reference at the top. Duplicate one sheet for each child.

Provide magazines and/or leftover take-home papers for the children to cut out pictures, or encourage them to draw their own original illustrations. Help the boys and girls paste or glue the pictures onto the sheets, then write their names when they are finished.

The parable Jesus told about the sower, found in Matthew 13:1-9, provides a good example of how to do a rebus story (illustrate all bold, capitalized words):

So many people wanted to hear **JESUS** one day that He got into a **BOAT** and talked to the people by the lake. Jesus told them a parable about a **FARMER** who went out to plant his garden.

Some of the **SEEDS** fell along the **PATH**, where the **BIRDS** came and ate them up.

Some of the **SEEDS** fell in between the **ROCKS**, where there wasn't much ground. Tiny plants grew, but when the **SUN** came up they wilted away.

Some of the **SEEDS** fell where the prickly **THORNS** are, but the plants

couldn't grow there because the thorns got so big.

But other **SEEDS** fell into the good ground, and they got plenty of **SUN** and **RAIN**. They grew into big, beautiful **PLANTS**.

Make sure that you not only tell the story to your students, but also explain to them what it means. In the parable told above, for example, you could say to the children that the seeds that fell and didn't grow are like people who hear about Jesus but don't ask Him to become their Savior. The seeds that grew, on the other hand, are like people who do ask Jesus to be their Savior and keep making choices to please Him.

Another idea:

Assign different verses to the older children and give them instructions to make the rebus craft at home. They can share their rebus stories with the class the following week.

9 Treasure Hunters

OBJECTIVE: To use the avenue of a "club" to encourage Bible reading and comprehension

Appropriate for ages 8 to 12

Children love to belong to clubs, so why not organize a Bible reading club for your students? Based on Isaiah 33:6, you can call it "Treasure Hunters."

This can be a special organization whose membership is dedicated to Bible reading. Let the children determine rules for membership — such as signing a pledge to read a certain number of verses, chapters or pages per week, giving a book report every few weeks, and so on. Emphasize to your class that membership in Treasure Hunters is a very special privilege that must be earned by willingness to uphold its rules and commitment to it objectives. Duplicate for the children the membership certificate on page 17 to hang on their bedroom walls and the membership cards to carry. (If desired, put a sticker like a gold seal in the bottom right corner of the certificate to make it look "official.")

Guide the children to elect officers; you may want to change often to give an opportunity for all students to eventually hold office. Collecting dues can be a simple way to purchase Bible-related books for the club library.

Use pre-session time in Sunday school, a block of time during children's church, or after school on a week day to hold regularly-scheduled meetings. These may consist of time for oral book reports; discussion of questions members may have about what they have read; craft time for making murals, models or displays depicting various stories or passages; creative writing time for paraphrasing or writing poems, plays, and stories about recent Bible-reading and the sharing of Scripture portions that Treasure Hunters memorize. Members can even reach out to others with a service project of recording Scripture portions or stories on cassette tapes to be used for

shut-ins or elderly visitation programs.

Invite special guests to speak to the group about experiences they have had connected with Bible-reading (the Gideons would be helpful with this), or to read to the students. Share stories about famous people who have used the Bible, such as George Washington. (At a time of crisis during the Revolutionary War, for instance, it is said that General Washington spent an entire day in church reading the Bible, praying and fasting.) Assign research projects for the members to complete between meetings, such as reports on Bible book authors, Bible background and customs, comparisons of different versions, etc.

Try to publish a regular report of happenings in your church newsletter, or let the students share with the congregation what is going on in the club. Publicity and recognition of the Treasure Hunters can help keep enthusiasm high.

TREASURE HUNTERS
Bible Reading Club
Isaiah 33:6

_____

is a member in good standing
Date _____

TREASURE HUNTERS
BIBLE READING CLUB

"And wisdom and knowledge shall be the stability of thy times, and strength of salvation: the fear of the Lord is His treasure."

Isaiah 33:6

_____

is a member in good standing of this organization, committed to its rules and objectives, and benefiting from its privileges.

_____   _____
Teacher   Date

---

10 ⬡ Bible Boxes

OBJECTIVE: To create a "special" place where children can specifically go to read the Bible

Appropriate for ages 7 to 10

The children in your class may find themselves more motivated to read their Bibles if they have a specific place to go for their devotion time. Help each student make his own "Bible Box" to take home for this purpose.

Ahead of class time, obtain large boxes from a grocery, appliance or furniture store. Cut away the top and one side. Let the children cut out pictures from old Sunday school take-home papers or magazines and tape or glue to the outside "walls" of their boxes. Encourage the children to use the interior walls as display space for Bible book reports, original pictures, and so on. The students may also ask their parents for an extra pillow to cushion the floor.

The finished box becomes a very personal place for the child to sit, in his bedroom or playroom, while reading the Bible.

11 How Do They Compare?

OBJECTIVE: To see the differences between the various versions of the Bible

Appropriate for age 9 to teens (and the entire congregation)

Comparing different versions of the Bible may help to make the Scriptures come alive to your students and become relevant to their lives now. It is important that children comprehend the meaning of Scripture in order to translate it into significant words they can use.

Obtain several versions of the Bible for the children to compare during class. These might include:

King James Version
New King James Version
Living Bible
Revised Standard Version
Amplified Bible
New International Version
New American Standard
Today's English Version

Explain to your students that although there is only one Bible, it was originally written in two different languages. Writers of the Old Testament spoke Hebrew, but by the time of Christ the people in that region talked and wrote in Greek. Very few people know Hebrew or Greek now, so the Bible has been put into our own language. The many different *versions* represent the variety of ways Scripture has been translated so that we can understand it better.

Duplicate the worksheet on page 19 so that each child has a copy. Direct the pupils to write across the top of the columns the different versions they will be using. Provide several Scripture references for the children to research, and tell them to write these in the first column of the worksheet.

The students can take turns using the different Bibles to find the Scriptures and write them in the various columns.

Ask the students to compare the versions to see the differences and similarities. Have them draw a circle around the version they like best and tell why for each of the Scripture selections. Allow time for class discussion of the various versions.

Some suggested verses are:
John 3:16
James 4:8
Matthew 11:28-30
Haggai 1:7
Acts 3:19

How Do They Compare?

Using several different versions of the Bible, look up the verses that your teacher gives you. Copy the verses onto this worksheet. Try to see the differences and similarities between them, then answer the questions below.

Scripture Reference _____	Version 1 _____	Version 2 _____	Version 3 _____	Version 4 _____

Which version do you like best? _____

Why did you choose that version? _____

12 — See What I Read

OBJECTIVE: To help children understand and communicate what they learn from the Bible

Appropriate for ages 8 to 12

In order to help your class members understand their Bible reading, provide an opportunity for them to "show" others what they learned from a particular passage.

Prepare slips of paper with Scripture references. These can be taken from your lesson material or randomly from the Bible. Provide each student with a sheet of construction paper or half a sheet of poster board. The children are to take these two items home, read the Scripture portion, then draw an illustration to show others what the Scripture said. Tell your students to bring the illustrations back the following week to share them with the rest of the class.

The following verses would be suitable for this learning activity: Psalm 119:105, Matthew 4:1-11, Mark 4:1-20, Exodus 19:16-21; 20:10-17, Daniel 3:19-25, Genesis 1:1-31, John 2:13-22, Mark 4:35-41, I Kings 18:30-39, and Acts 27:13-44.

13 — Keep 'em Guessing

OBJECTIVE: To challenge children to research facts in the Bible

Appropriate for age 9 to teens

Write on slips of paper the names of biblical characters or Bible stories and the Scripture references where they can be found. Put the slips in a bag and let each child in your class reach in to select one. Tell the students to take the slips home, look up the verse(s), and develop a list of statements about the Bible story or character.

Explain to the children that their clues will be used to play a guessing game with the class and that the following week they are to bring their "clues" to class. Allow time for each child to present his clues to the rest of the students. See who can keep the class guessing for the most number of clues.

14 Bible Story Placemats

OBJECTIVE: To help children comprehend what the Bible says

Appropriate for ages 4 to 9

After you have used several of the ideas in this book, your class should be familiar with a good number of Bible stories. Use this idea to help reinforce what the boys and girls have learned from those stories and to aid them in sharing their understanding with others.

Give each of your students a 12 by 18 inch piece of light-colored construction paper on which to make their placemats. Help them write the Scripture reference of a Bible story at the top, and provide crayons or felt-tip markers for the children to illustrate the story on the paper. The students may also wish to use stickers for decoration.

To complete the placemats, laminate or cover the drawings with adhesive-backed plastic. The children can take these home to use as reminders of their favorite Bible stories.

Another idea:

Let the children make extra placemats, perhaps even enough for their whole family. Encourage them to illustrate a different Bible story for each.

Designate a particular day when you will invite the parents of your class members to a "tea party." Bring a toaster to class and prepare enough slices of toast for the number of people you expect (unless you have adequate adult supervision, the children should wait until it is time to butter the slices to participate in the preparation). If so desired, the children may sprinkle on a mixture of sugar and cinnamon to make cinnamon toast or provide a variety of unique jams and jellies for the parents to sample. Provide juice or punch to drink.

Before the parents come in, ask the students to set the table using the placemats they made. When

it is time for the tea, the pupils may direct their parents to sit in the appropriate spot. Before the toast is served, each student may take a few minutes to tell his parents the Bible story, pointing out the various illustrations on the placemats. If your class is relatively small, you may choose to let each child tell about his placemat to the whole group. Even in the likelihood that some students will have the same Bible story, each child should have the opportunity to share in his own unique way.

After the tea, the children may take their placemats home. This might encourage family conversation about the Bible and/or lead to family Bible reading.

15 Books Within A Book

OBJECTIVE: To help children see that the books of the Bible are grouped into sections

Appropriate for age 6 to teens

The Bible may prove easier to understand if your students view it as many books within one. They are probably familiar with the idea of the Old and New testaments, but do they realize that these are also divided into particular sections? Explain the following to your class:

The first five books of the Old Testament — Genesis, Exodus, Leviticus, Numbers, and Deuteronomy — are called the Books of the Law. The Bible opens with the story of creation and then begins to tell about God's chosen people, the Israelites, and how God set the Law for them to live by.

The next twelve books—Joshua, Judges, Ruth, I and II Samuel, I and II Kings, I and II Chronicles, Ezra, Nehemiah, and Esther — are the Books of History. These tell about God's people living in their new homeland, then fighting and breaking into two nations, and finally both halves becoming slaves of their enemies in different countries.

Job, Psalms, Proverbs, Ecclesiastes, and the Song of Solomon make up the five Books of Poetry. Songs and poems praising God and wise sayings about how to live life are in these books.

The Books of the Major Prophets are Isaiah, Jeremiah, Lamentations, Ezekiel, and Daniel, while the Books of the Minor Prophets are Hosea, Joel, Amos, Obadiah, Jonah, Micah, Nahum, Habukkuk, Zephaniah, Haggai, Zechariah, and Malachi. When the people of Israel faced so much trouble, God sent messengers called prophets to remind them to obey the Lord and to look for their promised new King.

That King came in the New Testament. The first four books — Matthew, Mark, Luke, and John — are called the Gospels. They tell the Good News of Jesus' birth, the perfect life He lived, His death on the cross for our wrongdoing, and His coming back to life.

The next book, Acts, is another Book of History. It follows the lives of the people who knew about Jesus after He returned to heaven and how they helped others all over the world to become Christians.

The thirteen books that come after Acts are the Letters from Paul to those new Christians. Romans, I and II Corinthians, Galatians, Ephesians, Philippians, Colossians, and I and II Thessalonians were written to the brand new churches that Paul helped to start, while I and II Timothy, Titus, and Philemon were letters to individual people.

The next eight books — Hebrews; James; I and II Peter; I, II, and III John; and Jude — are also letters, but these were written by a number of different people. The General Letters encouraged the new believers to follow Jesus in the best possible way.

The last book is Revelation, a Book of Prophecy that tells how Jesus will someday come back to earth. The world as we know it will end, but Jesus will reign as King of a new world.

After the discussion time with your class, use the following crossword to help the lesson "sink in." Duplicate the puzzle on page 23 for each student. The boys and girls can use their Bibles to help find the correct answers.

Answers are on page 64.

Books Within A Book Crossword

Old Testament

LAW
Genesis
Exodus
Leviticus
Numbers
Deuteronomy

HISTORY
Joshua
Judges
Ruth
I Samuel
II Samuel
I Kings
II Kings
I Chronicles
II Chronicles
Ezra
Nehemiah
Esther

POETRY
Job
Psalms
Proverbs
Ecclesiastes
Song of Solomon

MINOR PROPHETS
Hosea
Joel
Amos
Obadiah
Jonah
Micah
Nahum
Habukkuk
Zephaniah
Haggai
Zechariah
Malachi

MAJOR PROPHETS
Isaiah
Jeremiah
Lamentations
Ezekiel
Daniel

New Testament

GOSPELS
Matthew
Mark
Luke
John

HISTORY
Acts

PAUL'S LETTERS
Romans
I Corinthians
II Corinthians
Galatians
Ephesians
Philippians
Colossians
I Thessalonians
II Thessalonians
I Timothy
II Timothy
Titus
Philemon

GENERAL LETTERS
Hebrews
James
I Peter
II Peter
I John
II John
III John
Jude

PROPHECY
Revelation

ACROSS

1. The last book of the law.
4. A letter in the New Testament that follows Hebrews.
5. A major prophet who wrote, "Unto us a Child is born, unto us a Son is given" (chapter 9, verse 6).
6. The Gospel that tells the Christmas story of the shepherds (chapter 2, verses 8-20).
9. The history book of the New Testament that tells about the first Christians.
13. A minor prophet in the Old Testament that follows Daniel.
14. An abbreviation for Paul's letters to the church at Thessalonica.
15. The second Gospel in the New Testament.
16. A book of history in the Old Testament that comes before Nehemiah.
17. The book of Israelite poetry and songs.

DOWN

1. A book written by a prophet who was thrown into a den of lions (chapter 6).
2. A history book named after a woman who stayed beside her mother-in-law.
3. A minor prophet book that comes between Amos and Jonah.
7. A history book named after a beautiful queen.
8. A minor prophet book that begins with the letter "A."
10. One of Paul's letters written to a Christian worker.
11. The Gospel that tells the story of the Wise Men (chapter 2, verses 1-12).
12. The first of Paul's letters.

16 Visualize The Bible

OBJECTIVE: To help younger children realize that Bible stories come from God's Word

Appropriate for ages 3 to 6

Obtain a large Bible that your preschool-aged children can handle for use in the classroom. Add a plastic jacket to the Bible for protection from little hands as well as for decoration.

Select pictures from your teaching aids or nursery and kindergarten Bible story papers. Place the pictures on sheets of paper the same size as the Bible and laminate or cover with clear adhesive-backed plastic. Secure the picture pages in the Bible where the stories appear, using clear tape along the binding.

Your students will love to "read" from their illustrated classroom Bible. In this way they will associate story with source and begin to enjoy the Bible even before learning to read.

17 Parent-Child Proverbs

OBJECTIVE: To help children see what the Bible says about parent-child relationships

Appropriate for ages 7 to 12

Many passages in the Book of Proverbs read like advice from a father to his son (this advice applies to daughters as well!). Others tell how a son or daughter should act toward his or her parents.

To help your students learn what the Bible has to say about parental instruction and discipline, direct them to some of these proverbs. Duplicate the worksheet on page 25 ahead of class time. Hand out one to each child and tell your students to look up the verses in their Bibles so they can fill in the blanks. When the boys and girls are finished, discuss with them ways that they can learn to accept their parents' discipline.

Answers are on page 64.

Parent-Child Proverbs

The following verses are all wise sayings from the Book of Proverbs (NIV) that talk about obeying our parents and making wise choices. Look up the references listed after each verse to help you fill in the blanks.

a. "Listen, my son, to your father's instruction and do not forsake your mother's teaching;. They will

be _____

_____." (Proverbs 1:8-9)

b. "A wise son brings joy to his father, but a foolish son _____

_____ ." (Proverbs 10:1)

c. "A wise son _____, but a mocker does not listen to

rebuke." (Proverbs 13:1)

d. "He who spares the rod hates his son, but he who loves him _____

_____." (Proverbs 13:24)

e. "He who ignores discipline despises himself, but whoever heeds correction _____

_____." (Proverbs 15:32)

f. "Listen to advice and accept instruction, and in the end _____."

(Proverbs 19:20)

g. "Train a child in the way he should go, and when he is old _____

_____ ." (Proverbs 22:6)

h. "My son, if your heart _____, then my heart will be glad." (Proverbs 23:15)

i. "My son, give me your heart and let your eyes _____."

(Proverbs 23:26)

j. "He who keeps the law is _____, but a companion of gluttons disgraces his

father." (Proverbs 28:7)

k. "He who robs his father or mother and says, 'It's not wrong,' — he is partner to him

_____." (Proverbs 28:24)

18 Who Knows?

OBJECTIVE: To help students motivate each other to find out what is in the Bible

Appropriate for age 7 to teens (and the entire congregation)

When you have a Sunday school party, use this Bible knowledge game to "break the ice."

Reproduce the Who Knows? box below for each participant. Tell the students to go around the room and ask each other who qualifies for the various categories. If someone can meet the description, he should sign his name on the appropriate line on his classmate's list. The one who finds the most people to fill in the blanks is the winner. However, each person who signed the winner's list should come before the rest of the class to prove he fits the description (for example, if one signed the line for being able to say the books of the Bible in order, he must come forward and quote them).

If the winner "loses" some of his answers, go to the student with the next highest number of signatures and direct the people on his list to come up. Continue until a "true" winner is found.

To check for accuracy, the answers or references to find them are as follows:

a. Answers will vary
b. Answers will vary
c. Look at Table of Contents in Bible
d. Psalm 23
e. Peter, James, John, Andrew, Philip, Bartholomew, Matthew, Thomas, James son of Alphaeus, Thaddaeus, Simon, and Judas (Mark 3:14-19)
f. Any four of Reuben, Simeon, Levi, Judah, Zebulun, Issachar, Dan, Gad, Asher, Naphtali, Joseph, and Benjamin (Genesis 49:3-28)
g. Saul, David, and Solomon (I Samuel 10:20-24, II Samuel 2:4-7, and I Kings 2:12)
h. Answers will vary
i. 1-light; 2-sky; 3-land, sea, and plants; 4-sun, moon, and stars; 5-fish and birds; 6-animals and man (Genesis 1:3-27)
j. Exodus 20:3-17

Who Knows?

a. Find someone with the name of a male Bible character. _____
b. Find someone with the name of a female Bible character. _____
c. Find someone who can say the books of the Bible in order. _____
d. Find someone who can quote Psalm 23. _____
e. Find someone who can name the twelve original apostles. _____
f. Find someone who can name four of the twelve tribes of Israel. _____
g. Find someone who can name the first three kings of Israel. _____
h. Find someone who can quote a whole chapter of the Bible. _____
i. Find someone who can say what God made on any one day of Creation. _____
j. Find someone who can name the Ten Commandments in order. _____

19 What Book?

OBJECTIVE: To review stories and Scriptures with a focus on where they are located

Appropriate for age 9 to teens (and the entire congregation)

Use this game at the end of a unit or any time after your students have become familiar with several Bible stories or passages of Scripture. The idea is to refresh their memories as well as point out what book the event or verse is from.

Write down on slips of paper the stories and Bible verses your students have been learning about and the books where they are located. Place the slips in an envelope or some other kind of container. Choose a leader to start by pulling out a slip and giving the clues. He may directly quote Scripture if he wishes. The student who first guesses the correct book becomes the new leader.

20 Found It!

OBJECTIVE: To help children become more familiar with the layout of the Bible

Appropriate for age 9 to teens (and the entire congregation)

Divide the class into several teams. Call out the Scripture references below to see which team can find the verse fastest. The first team member to locate a verse should say, "Found it!" and stand, making sure to keep his place so he can read the Scripture. If he has the correct verse, he wins one point for his team. After a given amount of time, see which team has the most points.

Some suggested Scriptures for this activity are: Psalm 119:11, Matthew 5:14, II Timothy 3:16, Deuteronomy 10:12, Psalm 24:8, Proverbs 22:1, I Peter 3:15, Ruth 1:16, Revelation 3:11, Exodus 15:2, Philippians 1:9, James 4:8, Zephaniah 3:17, and Micah 6:8.

Another idea:

Every member of the team must find the Scripture, then stand. The first team with all its members standing — with the correct reference — wins the point.

21 — God Will Do

OBJECTIVE: To show younger children that God keeps His promises

Appropriate for ages 3 to 5

Use this musical game to teach preschool children that God always does what He says He will do.

Direct your students to march around in a circle with one child standing in the middle. Sing the verses below to the tune of "Mulberry Bush." Stop at the end of each verse and ask if anyone knows who they are all singing about. The child in the middle may choose from among those who have their hands raised. If the child answers correctly, he may take the other's place in the middle.

You may of course create new verses using references to material your class has recently studied.

I see a rainbow in the sky, in the sky, in the sky.
I see a rainbow in the sky. God will do what
  He says.
Answer: Noah

I will go wherever He sends, wherever He sends, wherever He sends.
I will go wherever He sends. God will do what
  He says.
Answer: Abraham or Isaiah or apostles

I was saved from the lion's den, the lion's den, the lion's den.
I was saved from the lion's den. God will do what He says.
Answer: Daniel

22 God's Gift of Grace Bulletin Board

OBJECTIVE: To help children apply Bible teachings to their own lives

Appropriate for ages 6 to 9

To help your students better understand how grace affects our daily life, create a bulletin board focusing on what the Bible says about grace.

At the top of the board spell out the title, "God's Gift of Grace." Below it write Ephesians 2:8, "For by grace are ye saved through faith; and that not of yourselves: it is the gift of God."

Cut out construction paper rectangles and fold in half to make cards that open from top to bottom. On the inside write out Scriptures that pertain to grace and include the reference, then pin or staple to the bulletin board. Tape a gift-wrapping bow on the front flap. Your students can lift up the flaps to see what God's gift is all about.

Some possible references include:

Colossians 4:6, I Corinthians 15:10, Hebrews 4:16, Romans 5:15, and Acts 15:11.

23 The Names Of Jesus

OBJECTIVE: To encourage students to see the variety in the Bible's descriptive language

Appropriate for ages 8 to teens

Ask the children in your class to think of different names for Jesus. Can they think of five? or ten? The Bible uses more than 175 names for the Son of God (there's one)!

Challenge your students to spend time during the coming week reading their Bibles to see how many of those names they can find. Instruct the children to make a list of the names as well as the Scripture references where they were found. It will be fun to see who comes back the next week with the longest list of names. You might want to have a Bible concordance handy to check what the children find.

It would be appropriate to offer a small prize to the child who finds the most names for Jesus.

24 ⟨ Meet The Writer ⟩

OBJECTIVE: To show that God inspired many different people to write His Word

Appropriate for ages 8 to 12

Most books today include the name of the author on the front cover so everyone knows who wrote the book. This is not so with the Bible, so the children in your class may wonder exactly who is responsible for bringing us God's Word. Use this discussion guide and matching quiz to help your students understand where the Bible comes from.

Explain to your students that real people wrote the Bible. They ate and drank, slept and studied much like we do, but they lived in a time very different from ours. Computers, televisions, and VCRs did not exist. Even books as we know them today had not been invented yet. The only way for people to know what had happened in the past was if someone wrote down the events and passed this writing along for others to read.

As a result, the Bible is a collection of these writings from many different authors, passed from person to person. Eventually enough people read what the authors had to say that the decision came to gather all the writings into one book.

Read to your students II Timothy 3:16-17: "All Scripture is given by inspiration of God, and is profitable for doctrine, for reproof, for correction, for instruction in righteousness: that the man of God may be perfect, thoroughly furnished unto all good works." Tell your students that God knows which writings were included in the Bible; He helps us to understand the meaning of the history of His people and the life of His Son, and to apply that meaning to our lives.

Following the discussion time with your class, help the boys and girls find out who some of the

Bible's authors are. Ahead of class time, duplicate the matching quiz on page 31 for each child. Directions are on the sheet. Answers are on page 64.

Another idea:

After the children are finished with the matching game, ask them to choose a favorite book of the Bible and write a short letter to the author. Each student may include what he feels about things the author says and how reading that particular book is affecting his life. Encourage the children to share their letters with the class, then perhaps put the letters on display for others in the church to read.

Meet The Writer Matching Quiz

The statements below describe some of the Bible's authors and what they wrote about. Read through the list and then try to match the description with the person's name. Write the letter of the statement on the line next to the author's name. You may use your Bible to help find the answers.

1. _____ Paul
2. _____ Moses
3. _____ Daniel
4. _____ John
5. _____ Matthew
6. _____ David
7. _____ Luke
8. _____ Solomon

a. I led the Israelite people out of slavery in Egypt and served as their leader for many years. This story is told in the Book of Exodus, which I wrote along with Genesis, Leviticus, Numbers and Deuteronomy.

b. I was a doctor who traveled with Paul, telling people about Jesus. My book is the only Gospel that tells the story of the shepherds at Christ's birth. I also wrote the Book of Acts to show people what happened after Jesus went back to His Father in heaven.

c. As a young shepherd boy I killed a giant named Goliath; when I grew up I became King of Israel. I loved to praise God and tell Him my feelings, so I wrote most of the Book of Psalms.

d. When I first met Jesus, I was a tax collector. Although many people did not like me, Jesus called me to be one of His disciples and my heart changed. I wrote about His life so that people could see He was the promised King. My Gospel includes the story of the visit of the Magi.

e. My punishment for praying to God, which was against King Darius' orders, was to be thrown into the lion's den. When the king saw that God protected me, he praised the Lord. In my book I tell this story and one about three young men in a fiery furnace.

f. Although at first I tried to bring harm to the followers of Jesus, I became one myself and started traveling to other countries to tell others about Him. Many times I helped the new Christians form a church, then after I left I wrote letters to help them keep growing. These letters include: Romans, I and II Corinthians, Galatians, Ephesians, Philippians, Colossians, I and II Thessalonians, I and II Timothy, Titus, and Philemon.

g. I served as King of Israel after my father David. Since God gave me great wisdom, I wrote many sayings which became part of the Book of Proverbs. I also wrote about the meaning of life in the Book of Ecclesiastes, and a book of songs sometimes has my name in the title.

h. Known as the "disciple whom Jesus loved," I wrote a gospel about the miracles and teaching of Jesus and about His death and resurrection. Later I wrote three letters to help the younger believers who had never known Christ like I did. When God showed me things to happen in the end times, I wrote down what I saw in the Book of Revelation.

25 Roll Call Memory Rally

OBJECTIVE: To help children commit Scriptures to memory

Appropriate for ages 6 to 12

Start something new in your class for use when taking attendance. Invite your students to answer roll call by quoting a verse they have found in the Bible. They will of course have to find the Scriptures before they come to class, which should encourage them to read the Bible at home.

Tell your students that you will begin using the new way of taking roll the following week. If you wish, encourage the children to memorize verses that relate to your unit of study, such as creation or Jesus' parables, or verses that focus on one theme in particular, such as faith or salvation. Yet another idea is to learn verses all from one book; Psalms may be a good place to start.

For added interest, set up an attendance chart on the classroom wall. Use a Bible sticker by each child's name and write in the reference to the verse he quoted.

26 The Bible Tells Me So

OBJECTIVE: To help children make a visual reminder of what the Bible says to them

Appropriate for ages 3 to 6

Since most preschool-aged children do not know how to read, your younger students may need more visual reinforcement to understand what God's Word says to them. To emphasize the Bible's message of love, help your students make the following craft.

First tell your class the Bible story of Jesus and the children found in Matthew 19:13-15. Then give each child a sheet of black construction paper and show the students how to fold the paper in the center to make a book cover. Provide a sheet of white paper to put inside, on which you have printed, "Jesus loves me this I know, for the Bible tells me so." In place of the first "me" you may want to print the child's name. Help the children punch holes along the left edge and use a piece of yarn to tie the "Bible" together.

27 "Chute" For Your Best

OBJECTIVE: To encourage the practice of regular Bible reading

Appropriate for ages 6 to 12

Set a goal of a specific number of Bible books or chapters to be read by a certain date. Prepare a large bulletin board where the children can keep track of their progress with "parachutes" that they make in craft time. The boys and girls will have fun as they "chute" for their best and try to reach the goal.

Show each child how to make a mini-parachute out of wallpaper samples or scrap fabric and pieces of string. Then help the students cut out small human shapes and color on some clothes. Each child may write his name on the shape or bring a small picture of himself and cut out his face to glue onto the figure's head. Attach the parachutes and figures to the top of the board with pins or Plasti-tac so they can be easily moved. As the children make progress toward the goal, their parachutes will "float" down.

28 It's Time To Read Bulletin Board

OBJECTIVE: To spark an interest in reading Bible stories

Appropriate for ages 6 to 12

An unusual alarm clock on this bulletin board signals children to read the Bible. You may use this idea in several ways: to illustrate your present unit of study, to review lessons previously taught, or simply to motivate your students to take the time to discover what interesting things the Bible has to offer.

Cut out a large poster board alarm clock. In place of numbers, use pictures illustrating various stories found in the Bible. Left-over teaching aids or take-home papers are a good source for these. Cut clock hands out of black construction paper and attach them to the poster board with a paper fastener so they can be moved for added interest.

Using pre-cut letters or ones that you make yourself out of colorful construction paper, spell out the words "It's Time To Read The Bible" on the bulletin board and position the clock underneath.

29 Who Said That?

Appropriate for ages 8 to 12

To help your students realize that the Bible tells us about real people and real situations, let them research the Scriptures to see what some of those people said. Read each verse and reference to the class, then see who finds the answer first. (You may need to tell the students to read the surrounding verses to find out who was speaking). Allow time after each question for discussion about the circumstances or the person.

a. "Now therefore be not grieved, nor angry with yourselves, that ye sold me hither: for God did send me before you to preserve life." Genesis 45:5 (Joseph)
b. "Who am I, that I should go unto Pharoah, and that I should bring forth the children of Israel out of Egypt?" Exodus 3:11 (Moses)
c. "Speak; for Thy servant heareth." I Samuel 3:10 (Samuel)
d. "Take me up, and cast me forth into the sea; so shall the sea be calm unto you: for I know that for my sake this great tempest is upon you." Jonah 1:12 (Jonah)
e. "Create in me a clean heart, O God; and renew a right spirit within me." Psalm 51:10 (David)
f. "If I have found favor in thy sight, O king, and if it please the king, let my life be given me at my petition, and my people at my request." Esther 7:3 (Esther)
g. "Behold, this child is set for the fall and rising again of many in Israel." Luke 2:34 (Simeon)
h. "I am the voice of one crying in the wilderness." John 1:23 (John the Baptist)
i. "If thou wilt, let us make here three tabernacles; one for Thee, and one for Moses, and one for Elias." Matthew 17:4 (Peter)
j. "Thou couldest have no power at all against Me, except it were given thee from above." John 19:11 (Jesus)
k. "Behold, I see the heavens opened, and the Son of Man standing on the right hand of God." Acts 7:56 (Stephen)
l. "Understandeth thou what thou readeth?" Acts 8:30 (Philip)
m. "Lord, they know that I imprisoned and beat in every synagogue them that believed on Thee." Acts 22:19 (Paul)

30 Scripture Search

OBJECTIVE: To help students learn to use the topical method to study God's Word

Appropriate for age 9 to teens

Sometimes when we are studying a particular story or Scripture, we limit our learning to just a few verses. On many occasions, however, the Bible has much more to say about a subject, and usually the other Scriptures are scattered throughout both testaments. But how do we find them without reading every page? We use the topical Bible study method.

Help your children learn to use this valuable method by providing opportunities for topical research and study. You will need to bring a concordance or topical Bible to class (often the students' Bibles will have a small concordance in the back). To focus on a particular subject, look up the key word in the concordance and see if other Scriptures that relate to the subject are listed.

As an example, if you are studying Jesus' parable of the mustard seed, ask the children to look up the word "faith" in their concordances. They will find several verses listed in the order in which they are found in the Bible. Invite each child to read a few different verses to the class. See how much more they understand about faith after reading the various Scriptures.

Discuss with your students how topical Bible study can help them when they are hurting, afraid,

lonely, upset, or experiencing other needs or problems. They can also use the topical method when they are full of joy and just want to praise the Lord. Ask for suggestions of topics to study, then have the children look in their concordances to find Scriptures concerning these areas.

31 Bible Blocks Bulletin Board

OBJECTIVE: To create a 3-D interest center that encourages children to read the Bible

Appropriate for age 3 to 12

Let loose your creativity — build a four-sided display bulletin board for your room. This will take some time to prepare, but it is an excellent interest and discussion center.

Obtain at least three boxes, each of a different size, and cover each with a different color of construction paper or adhesive-backed plastic. Stack the boxes one on top of the other with the largest one on the bottom.

Gather leftover teaching aids or take-home papers to cut out pictures. Since this "bulletin board" offers more space than usual, a good idea might be to illustrate a particular book of the Bible. Tape or glue the pictures on each side of all the boxes to illustrate what you wish. Put the pictures in order from top to bottom so that the last picture on the bottom box is the last story from the book you want to emphasize.

32 Paul's Letters Puzzle

OBJECTIVE: To focus on the letters by Paul as part of the inspired Word of God

Appropriate for age 9 to teens

Nearly half of our New Testament consists of letters written by the Apostle Paul to the people of his day. These letters are still relevant to us today though, for as II Timothy 3:16 says, all Scripture "is profitable for doctrine, for reproof, for correction, for instruction in righteousness."

Explain to your class that the Book of Acts tells how Paul came to know Jesus as his Savior and then traveled as a missionary. With several helpers, Paul started churches in many cities around the world. He then wrote letters to those churches and to certain people, mostly to teach them to make the right choices and to give encouragement.

Help your class see what kinds of things Paul wrote in his letters. Duplicate the puzzle on page 37 for each student. Encourage the children to try to memorize one of the verses.

Answers are on page 64.

Paul's Letters Puzzle

The following verses are taken from Paul's letters to the people and churches he worked with. Those letters make up part of our New Testament. The chapter and verse are provided; use your Bible (NIV) to try to find out the correct book. Write down the names of the books on the dash lines.

a.   (2:5) "Your attitude should be the same as that of Christ Jesus."

b.   (5:17) "Therefore, if anyone is in Christ, he is a new creation; the old has gone, the new has come!"

c.   (2:11) "For the grace of God that brings salvation has appeared to all men."

d.   (5:22-23) "But the fruit of the Spirit is love, joy, peace, patience, kindness, goodness, faithfulness, gentleness and self-control. Against such things there is no law."

e.   (6:11) "Put on the full armor of God so that you can take your stand against the devil's schemes."

f.   (5:18) "Give thanks in all circumstances, for this is God's will for you in Christ Jesus."

g.   (6) "I pray that you may be active in sharing your faith, so that you will have a full understanding of every good thing we have in Christ."

h.   (4:12) "Don't let anyone look down on you because you are young, but set an example for the believers in speech, in life, in love, in faith, and in purity."

i.   (13:13) "And now these three remain: faith, hope and love. But the greatest of these is love."

j.   (3:3) "But the Lord is faithful, and he will strengthen and protect you from the evil one."

k.   (12:1) "Therefore, I urge you, brothers, in view of God's mercy, to offer your bodies as living sacrifices, holy and pleasing to God — this is your spiritual act of worship."

l.   (3:20) "Children, obey your parents in everything, for this pleases the Lord."

a.   P _ _ _ _ _ _ _ _

b.   _ _ _ _ _ _ _ _ _ A _ _

c.   _ _ _ U _

d.   _ _ L _ _ _ _ _ _

e.   _ _ _ _ S _ _ _ _

f.   _ _ _ _ _ _ _ L _ _ _ _ _ _

g.   _ _ _ _ E _ _ _

h.   _ _ _ _ _ T _ _

i.   _ _ _ _ _ _ T _ _ _ _ _

j.   _ _ _ E _ _ _ _ _ _ _ _ _ _

k.   R _ _ _ _ _

l.   _ _ _ _ S _ _ _ _ _

33 Bible Reading Marathon

OBJECTIVE: To spark an interest in Bible reading in a fun and informal manner

Appropriate for age 10 to teens

This activity would work well as part of a retreat, "lock-in" or some other time when there will be a group of students together over a period of two or three days. It could also be presented by the youth group at a local shopping mall to attract attention to Bible reading.

You may want to designate certain chapters to be read, or if the group is large enough, determine that you'll read the entire Bible from cover to cover. Ask your students to sign up to read Scripture for 15, 30 or 60 minutes at a time. On the specified day, start the marathon at 8:00 or 9:00 in the morning — with much fanfare and publicity — and continue the entire day until 4:00 or 5:00 in the afternoon. Older students might want to keep on reading until later in the evening; the pupils can pick up the next day where they left off.

Remember to plan for meals for your students. Tell them to bring a sack lunch and some munchies, or ask members of the congregation if they would like to provide food. The adults would probably enjoy the opportunity to help with the activity, especially for such a "worthy cause."

The success of the Bible Reading Marathon will depend upon the enthusiasm that you can create beforehand. Invite the public to come and watch the progress. Prepare a bulletin board or chalkboard so that "scorekeepers" can keep track of how much the group has read. Perhaps at the end of each book the children could make a special musical presentation. Invite the local newspaper or television station to cover the event, and urge members of the congregation to be on hand to offer support and encouragement to the youngsters.

Another idea:

Make the purpose two-fold by using the marathon as a fund raiser. Give the students a

sign up sheet to ask for sponsors who will contribute a certain amount of money per the amount of time or number of books read. This can be another way to get the public involved if the students go to their teachers, parents of friends, and neighbors for help.

At the end of the marathon, verify for each student what he has done and perhaps sign a certificate for him to show his sponsors. Set a specific date when all the money should be in (if any students have trouble collecting from a sponsor or two, tell them not to worry about it).

Depending on the needs of your church, you may decide to donate the money to the missions fund or to a building project. Your students may want to purchase Bibles to send to other children who need them. The possibilities are endless— invite your class to brainstorm with you and choose together.

34 I'm Thinking Of A Verse

OBJECTIVE: To help children learn how to use a concordance

Appropriate for age 9 to teens (and the entire congregation)

How many times can you remember just part of a verse, or even just one word, and you want to read the entire verse? In order to help children learn to find verses when such an occasion arises, use this Bible concordance drill.

Explain to your class that a concordance is "a dictionary of words or phrases, with references to the places where they occur in the Bible." Several different concordances, ranging from a large exhaustive publication to a small pocket one, should be on hand for illustration and use.

Show the children how to use the concordances much like they would a dictionary. Then begin the drill by giving clues, using just a few key words from the verse they are to find. Tell the children to turn to the verse in their Bibles after they have found it in the concordance. The first one to locate the Scripture should stand and read the verse. Try to let every child have a chance to read one of the verses.

Some possible Scriptures for the children to locate are:

a. "My grace is sufficient for thee: for My strength is made perfect in weakness." (II Corinthians 12:9a)

b. "The eternal God is thy refuge, and underneath are the everlasting arms." (Deuteronomy 33:27a)

c. "And I will make them and the places round about my hill a blessing; and I will cause the shower to come down in his season; there shall be showers of blessing." (Ezekiel 34:26)

d. "Ho, every one that thirsteth, come ye to the waters." (Isaiah 55:1a)

e. "I am Alpha and Omega, the Beginning and the Ending, saith the Lord, which is, and which was, and which is to come, the Almighty." (Revelation 1:8)

f. "The heavens declare the glory of God; and

OH, THAT'S HOW THE VERSE GOES!

the firmament showeth His handiwork." (Psalm 19:1)

g. "Take My yoke upon you, and learn of Me; for I am meek and lowly in heart: and ye shall find rest unto your souls." (Matthew 11:29)

h. "Which hope we have as an anchor of the soul, both sure and stedfast, and which entereth into that within the veil." (Hebrews 6:19)

i. "But ye are a chosen generation, a royal priesthood, an holy nation, a peculiar people; that ye should show forth the praises of Him who hath called you out of darkness into His marvellous light." (I Peter 2:9)

j. "Though He slay me, yet will I trust in Him." (Job 13:15a)

Another idea:

Have a concordance drill called "Where Am I?" where you begin to read a passage in the Bible and continue until a student locates the verses by using a concordance.

35 ⬡ Pick And Choose

OBJECTIVE: To help children remember where basic Bible passages are found

Appropriate for ages 8 to 12

This is a game that will help your students learn where various stories and passages are found in the Bible.

You will need two sets of twelve 5 by 7 inch cards. Letter one set: The Ten Commandments; The Beatitudes; The Lord's Prayer; The Fall of Jericho; Prodigal Son Parable; Good Samaritan Parable; Lazarus Raised Miracle; Creation; Walking on the Sea Miracle; Lost Sheep Parable; Sower Parable; and Five Thousand Fed Miracle.

Letter the second set: Exodus 20:1-17; Matthew 5:3-12; Matthew 6:9-13; Joshua 5:13-6:27; Luke 15:11-32; Luke 10:25-37; John 11:1-44; Genesis 1-2; Mark 6:47-52; Luke 15:3-7; Mark 4:1-20; and Mark 6:35-44.

To play, let a student "pick" a card from the first set. Next have him "choose" from the second set (spread out so all references are visible) to try to match passage and reference.

36 ⬡ Bible Caravan

OBJECTIVE: To visually reinforce Bible lessons in a creative format

Appropriate for ages 8 to 12

Help your students learn what can be found in the different books of the Bible by putting up a Bible "caravan" around the walls of your classroom.

Duplicate the camel patterns on page 41 so that you have plenty of camels to represent the stories and events that are recorded in the Bible. During pre-session or activity time in class, assign the children to cover different books from the Bible. Ask each student to look through the book and prepare a camel for each main event by printing the name of the story, names of main characters, etc., and the Scripture reference. Since some books contain more of the well-known stories than others, such as Genesis or the Gospels, you may want to focus the theme of the caravan around just one book. When the camels are finished, fasten them to the wall in a line around the room.

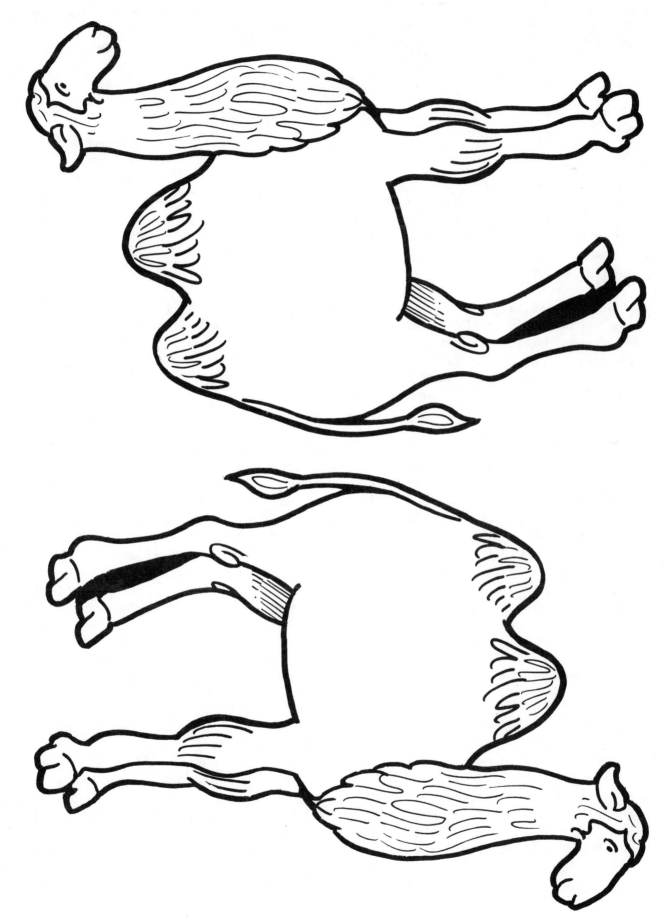

37 How The Bible Came To Be

OBJECTIVE: To help children understand the origin of the Bible

Appropriate for ages 6 to 12

Of all the books that have ever been written, more people read and learn from the Bible than from any other book. Why? Because this book reveals God's plan for our salvation through Christ. But where did the Bible come from? No doubt your students have asked this question at one time or another. Use this activity to take them back through the ages and trace the Bible's journey to us. Explain the following information to the children:

"People were living on earth for hundreds of years before any part of the Bible was written. Writing had not been invented, but God spoke to people through His creation and He spoke to people directly. These people shared God's message to others through the spoken word. By Moses' time the alphabet had been invented (around 1400 to 1200 B.C.) and he was able to put these messages from God into the written word. However, few people knew how to read or write and still continued to just tell the stories of God and His people to their children.

"Some people did go to school and learned to become scribes, or what we might call secretaries. The stories and psalms were told to them to be put into writing. Paper had not yet been invented, so they used pieces of the papyrus plant which were dried and pressed flat. The papyrus writings were rolled up into scrolls. Since the papyrus scrolls wore out from their continued use, the scribes had to keep making new copies. Each scroll had to be carefully copied by hand — there were no typewriters or computers in those days.

"Most of the Old Testament scrolls were written in Hebrew, which was the scribes' native language. But when the people of Israel were forced to live in Babylon, they learned a new language — Aramaic — and some of the last books of the Old Testament were written in that language. Around 300 B.C. the Greeks conquered Israel and its neighbors and most of the people learned to speak Greek. The books of the New Testament were written in the Greek language.

"Not too long after the time of the apostles, someone invented the codex, which was a book with pages. The scrolls had been heavy and the person reading from them had to do a lot of unrolling. This made it necessary for the scrolls to be short, which meant that there had to be many dozens of scrolls. It was nearly impossible to carry them around from place to place. Now, with the codex, it was possible to have God's Word written on individual pages that could be put into a book like we recognize today. However, those books were quite heavy because the pages were made out of animal skins, many times thicker than paper, so the Bibles were about a foot thick. Those Bibles were also very expensive, and because it took so long to hand print each copy, they were usually only placed in synagogues where people came to hear the Scriptures read.

"These early Bibles were made by monks, men who have devoted themselves to serving God and who spend part of their time closely studying the Scriptures. Usually one monk would read the Bible while five or six others carefully wrote down what he read. These copies were checked very carefully and if a mistake was found, that entire copy was destroyed. Just imagine how long it would take to copy each word of the Bible by hand and then check each word for errors.

"The early Bibles were so expensive, they had to be chained to a desk to keep thieves from stealing them. Finally, paper and printing presses were invented so that thousands of Bibles can be printed at once. Now most people can have their own Bible, and many have more than one."

To help your students visualize what the early forms of Scripture might have looked like, use the following activity at the end of the lesson: invite the children to pretend to be scribes and make their own hand-printed copies of some Bible verses.

First, choose a verse and direct the pupils to copy it very carefully on a sheet of paper. Tell them to go back afterwards and check for accuracy. Next, the students should again copy the verse, leaving out all the vowels and printing backwards from right to left. Explain that this was the way much of the Old Testament was written. Finally the students should print the verse a third time, but leave no spaces between the words and use only capital letters. This is similar to how the New Testament was originally written.

For classes with younger students who do not yet have a good grip on writing, you might want to simply do the activity yourself and show them

the finished verses.

When the class is finished with the writing activity, pray together, offering thanks to God that we have modern inventions to make it possible for each of us to have our very own copy of His Word.

38 The Bible Around The World

OBJECTIVE: To show children that God's Word is for people of all languages

Appropriate for age 10 to teens (and the entire congregation)

Unless your students come from a bilingual home or have friends and neighbors who speak other languages, it is very probable that they tend to believe English is the only language spoken. Even if they are told otherwise in, say, a missionary service, the children are not likely to understand the concept of differing languages without seeing or hearing it for themselves.

Explain to your class that people read and write different languages depending usually on where they were born and grew up. Ask your students to raise their hands if they were born in another country. If you have any positive responses, ask the children to say a few words in the language of that country.

Tell the boys and girls that the Bible was originally written in both Hebrew and Greek, and then years later it was put into other languages for the rest of the world to read. No matter what language it is written in, though, God's Word is always true.

One of the most familiar Scriptures worldwide is John 3:16, for it is the "Gospel in a nutshell." Use this verse to help your students see the difference between English and three other common languages. Place a sheet of paper over this half of the page so that you can duplicate the bottom half for the boys and girls. Invite the children to try to sound out the words; they of course will not pronounce the words correctly, but the exercise

will at least help them see first-hand what another language looks like.

If possible, you might ask the congregation if anyone knows another language and invite that person to visit your class. Ask your guest to read the verse to the students and answer any questions about the country that they might have. If your guest has any souvenir-type items, encourage him to bring them to show the class as well. Take the idea further and make it part of a missionary study or special meal; you can choose from a number of possibilities.

God's Word Is For Everyone

English
"For God so loved the world, that He gave His only begotten Son, that whosoever believeth in Him should not perish, but have everlasting life."
John 3:16

French
"Car Dieu a tant aimé le monde qu'il a donné son Fils unique, afin que quiconque croit en lui ne périsse pas, mais qu'il ait la vie éternelle."
Jean 3:16

German
"Denn also hat Gott die Welt geliebt, daß er seinen eingebornen Sohn gab, auf daß alle, die an ihn glauben, nicht verloren werden, sondern das ewige Leben haben."
Johannes 3:16

Spanish
Porque de tal manera amó Dios al mundo, que ha dado a su Hijo unigénito, para que todo aquel que en él cree, no se pierda, mas tenga vida eterna.
San Juan 3:16

39 Diving For Treasure Game

OBJECTIVE: To familiarize children with God's Word through a fun and exciting game

Appropriate for ages 6 to 12

This game will encourage children to "dive" into their Bibles to find the wonderful treasures God has for them. The treasures they will find in the Bible are not silver and gold, but words that are much more valuable. Silver and gold will not last, but the Word of God can never be spent or lost. Its value never changes. We can learn Scripture and keep it in our hearts and minds to be used at any time and any place where it is needed. The Word of God brings comfort, endurance, help, encouragement, strength, compassion and love.

The Diving for Treasure game will help children see how God has worked in the lives of other people and that He is always ready to work in their lives if they just trust and obey.

To play the game, first duplicate the game board on page 46 (you may color and laminate it if you wish) and tape or glue to the inside of a manila folder. You may create questions for this game out of your present unit of study, or use the general Bible questions included on pages 47-50. Duplicate the questions, laminate, and cut apart to make question/answer cards. Tape a 2 by 3 inch construction paper rectangle at the top of the game board to make a pocket for the cards.

Duplicate the markers at the bottom of this page, making one for each child. The players will take turns answering the questions. If a student answers the question correctly without using his Bible, he may dive two levels down into the sea. If he needs to look up an answer in his Bible, allow only forty-five to sixty seconds for him to find the

Scripture. If he finds the answer within that time limit, he can dive one level down into the sea. Players make no dive if they give no answer or if it is incorrect.

For added enthusiasm, if the player taking a turn cannot give an answer or locate the answer in the Bible within the allotted time period, the next player can try to answer the question. Such an answer will permit that player to dive only one level. Discard the question if no one can answer it after three players have tried.

The first player to reach the treasure at the bottom of the game board wins.

Diving
For
Treasure

Tape a 2 by 3 inch construction paper rectangle here for the question/answer cards

Start

Level 1

Level 2

Level 3

Level 4

Level 5

Treasure Chest

God's Word

Who was called "the dreamer" by his brothers?

What did God provide for the hungry Israelites in the wilderness?

What great walled city fell at the sound of the trumpets and the shout of the people?

Who was the rich publican who because of his little stature climbed a tree in order to see Jesus?

Who in a dream saw a ladder reaching from earth to heaven?

Who said to himself, "I will arise and go to my father?

How many men were seen walking unharmed in the fiery furnace?

God sent a prophet to Nineveh, but the man took a ship to Tarshish instead. Who was he?

To what city was Paul traveling when he saw a great light and heard the voice of Jesus?

Who showed his friendship to David by giving him gifts?

Who put out the fleece of wool to test the will of the Lord?

What was the serpent in the Garden of Eden condemned to eat all the days of its life?

How long was Jesus in the wilderness, tempted by the devil?

For what act was Daniel thrown into the lion's den?

What king was famed for his great wisdom and magnificent kingdom?

Jericho (Joshua 6:2-5)	Manna (Exodus 16:15)	Joseph (Genesis 37:17b-19)
The Prodigal (younger) Son (Luke 15:18)	Jacob (Genesis 28:10-12)	Zacchaeus (Luke 19:2-4)
Damascus (Acts 9:1-3)	Jonah (Jonah 1:1-3)	Four (Daniel 3:25)
Dust (Genesis 3:14)	Gideon (Judges 6:36-37)	Jonathan (I Samuel 18:3-4)
Solomon (I Kings 10)	Praying (Daniel 6:10-12)	Forty days (Luke 4:1-2)

Who said to Jesus, "Lord, remember me when Thou comest into Thy kingdom?"

What is the Word of God called in the Christian's armor?

In Romans 12:1, what did Paul tell the Romans they were to do with their bodies?

What is possible with God?

Jesus said they are blessed who hunger and thirst after what?

What will God give us if we delight ourselves in the Lord?

What did Jesus tell us not to love?

II Corinthians 12:9 says what is sufficient for us?

What are we to overcome evil with?

Jesus said if we believe on Him we will have what?

What is the Son of Man come to seek and to save?

What is the first and great commandment?

What is the second commandment Jesus told us?

What will Jesus give to those who labor and are heavy laden, if they come to Him?

Who was miraculously released from prison by an angel?

"Present your bodies a living sacrifice, holy, acceptable unto God."

"The sword of the Spirit"
(Ephesians 6:17)

The second thief on the cross
(Luke 23:39-42)

The desires of our hearts
(Psalm 37:4)

Righteousness
(Matthew 5:6)

All things
(Mark 10:27)

Overcome evil with good
(Romans 12:21)

"My grace is sufficient for thee."

"Love not the world, neither the things that are in the world."
(I John 2:15)

"Thou shalt love the Lord thy God with all thy heart, and with all thy soul, and with all thy mind."
(Matthew 22:37-38)

That which is lost
(Luke 19:10)

Everlasting life
(John 6:47)

Peter
(Acts 12:7)

Rest
(Matthew 11:28)

"Thou shalt love thy neighbor as thyself."
(Matthew 22:39)

40 Talking Mural

OBJECTIVE: To help children express to others what they have learned from the Bible

Appropriate for ages 6 to 12

Use a "talking mural" as a unique presentation for your class to make during opening exercises or a special program at church. The mural will help the children to both visualize and verbalize Bible lessons, thus making them more real.

Secure a long sheet of butcher paper to the wall for the children to create the mural. Provide crayons or colored pencils (markers if your students can handle them well) and direct the children to draw, life-size if possible, the various people they learned about in a recently taught Bible lesson.

After the mural is drawn, cut out the faces of the Bible characters. For the presentation, designate a couple of children to hold the mural up so that other children can sit behind it. These students will then become the "faces" of the biblical characters and tell, in their own words, their stories.

41 The Bible Describes God

OBJECTIVE: To help children find out what kind of words the Bible uses to portray God

Appropriate for ages 6 to 9

Talk with the children in your class about what they think of God. Who is He? What is He like? How can we know whether He is really faithful or loving or gentle?

Say to your students that the Bible tells us many things about God. In virtually every story, every event, we can read something that describes Who God really is.

Duplicate the crossword puzzle on page 52 for each child. Let the students use their Bibles to find the correct words.

Answers:
1. JUST
2. FAITHFUL
3. HOLY
4. ALMIGHTY
5. MERCIFUL
6. LIVING
7. STRONG
8. KIND
9. EVERLASTING
10. TRUE
11. PERFECT
12. FORGIVING

The Bible Describes God

1. God is _ _ _ _ (I John 1:9)
2. God is _ _ _ _ _ _ _ _ (I Corinthians 1:9)
3. God is _ _ _ _ (Revelation 4:8)
4. God is _ _ _ _ _ _ _ _ (Genesis 17:1)
5. God is _ _ _ _ _ _ _ _ (Nehemiah 9:31)
6. God is _ _ _ _ _ _ (Deuteronomy 5:26)
7. God is _ _ _ _ _ _ (Psalm 24:8)
8. God is _ _ _ _ (Luke 6:35)
9. God is _ _ _ _ _ _ _ _ _ _ (Isaiah 40:28)
10. God is _ _ _ _ (John 17:3)
11. God is _ _ _ _ _ _ _ (II Samuel 22:31)
12. God is _ _ _ _ _ _ _ _ _ (Exodus 34:6-7)

42 Weekday Bible Scavenger Hunt

OBJECTIVE: To encourage children to read their Bibles at home

Appropriate for ages 8 to 12

Use this idea of a scavenger hunt to motivate your students to do some biblical "research" on their own. Cover half this sheet to duplicate the following list of Scripture references, and provide a paper sack for each child. Tell the pupils to look up the verses to figure out what the various items are, then try to find as many of the items as possible. (Younger children may need a little help from their parents with the household items.) The students should bring their sacks to class the following week to see who found the most items.

Answers:

a. Five smooth stones
b. Seeds
c. Sand
d. Salt
e. Scarlet (red) thread
f. Grass
g. Branch
h. Piece of money
i. Shoes
j. Dust
k. Soap

Bible Scavenger Hunt

a. What David put in his shepherd's bag when he prepared to fight Goliath (I Samuel 17:40)
b. Some fell by the wayside, some in stony places, some among the thorns, and some into good ground (Matthew 13:4-8)
c. What the foolish man built his house upon (Matthew 7:26)
d. Somewhere near Sodom and Gomorrah there is some of this substance (Genesis 19:26)
e. Rahab put this in her window (Joshua 2:18)
f. Nebuchadnezzar ate this (Daniel 4:33)
g. Christ is the vine and we are the_____ (John 15:5)
h. Jesus told Peter he would find this in the mouth of a fish (Matthew 17:27)
i. What the father put on the feet of his Prodigal Son (Luke 15:22)
j. God used this to form man (Genesis 2:7)
k. "For He is like a refiner's fire, and like fullers' _____" (Malachi 3:2)

43 Improvisational Bible Theater

OBJECTIVE: To actively involve children in the telling of Bible stories

Appropriate for ages 4 to 12

A well-known comedian has said, "Everybody wants to get into the act." Children are no exception. As the ideal learning situation allows a child's imagination to work as a part of the educating process, improvisational theater is a wonderful method to get students into their work of learning. It is an excellent way to help reinforce the meaning of a Bible story.

When a child can play Moses, Elijah, or one of Jesus' disciples, he will remember their roles in the Bible for a longer period of time than otherwise would be expected. When he plays David, he learns a deeper appreciation for a shepherd and hence for The Good Shepherd.

Improvisational theater can take as little or as much preparation as you wish to put into it. A good idea to always include, however, is to list for yourself all the characters who will be involved and write their names on colorful strips of construction paper for the students to hold. This will not only keep track of who's who, but it will also help the children identify more quickly with what is going on. You may also want to use large grocery bags for costumes. Cut out holes for the arms and head and color with crayons or felt-tip markers.

Always enter into story play with a great deal of enthusiasm — it will catch on! Say to your students that you need help with telling the Bible story and ask for volunteers. Explain to the boys and girls that they should act out what is happening as you tell the story.

Improvise with anything you can get your hands on. Chairs can become trees or chariots or

whatever you want them to be. Substitute the rug for a throne, a bed, or a lake.

Use sound effects to add to the story. Stomp feet for footsteps. Ask a student to crumple paper for the sound of fire. Another can whistle like the wind. Turn your whole class into galloping horses (first clap hands together, then quickly slap a leg with one hand, then the other.)

The only hard-and-fast rule with improvisational theater is for both you and your students to enjoy the activity. Be as creative as you can to help your students understand more about what the Bible teaches us. They will remember these lessons.

44 Sermon On The Mount . . . Live!

OBJECTIVE: To help children focus on the reality of the Bible

Appropriate for age 10 to teens (and the entire congregation)

Plan an experimental Bible study for your children by helping them to "experience" Bible times as if they were actually there. In this activity they will pretend they are among the crowd as Jesus preaches the Sermon on the Mount.

Provide cassette recorders for various members of your class and assign them to go out and record background sounds for your Bible study. They should record such sounds as footsteps, birds singing, a running stream, noisy crowds, etc. Ask one older student (or perhaps an adult) to record in his own voice Christ's words from the Sermon on the Mount (Matthew 5:3-7:27), and another child to record the narration to set the scene (Matthew 5:1-2 and 7:28-29). Make a master recording of everything, with the background sounds worked into the narration and the reading of the Scripture.

If possible, present this Bible study in a large, uncluttered room that can be overheated a bit to create an Israeli atmosphere, and maybe have a few fans going to create a hot breeze in the room. It would also add to the presentation to build a "mountain" at one end of the room by draping dark fabric over chairs that are stacked on top of tables. Darken the room just a bit to create an awesome appearance.

When the students enter the room, ask them to imagine they are walking down a dirt road in Israel on their way to see Jesus. When they are all seated (on the floor), ask them to close their eyes and listen as "Jesus" preaches the Sermon on the Mount.

At the end of the presentation, ask your students what they think of Jesus' teachings. Is there an idea that sticks in their minds the most? How difficult or easy would it be to live the way Jesus says to?

Try to help the students focus on present-day situations, such as when a classmate at school insults them or someone keeps getting into their desk. Could they rejoice in the midst of persecution? Could they forgive and forget?

Allow for a quiet time of reflection for the students to think about how Jesus' teaching should affect their lives. The presentation will hopefully serve as a catalyst for some thought on the matter.

45 Scripture Scrolls

OBJECTIVE: To help children appreciate how the Bible came to us

Appropriate for ages 6 to 8

Lend an air of authenticity to Bible reading: make scrolls resembling those from long ago.

First explain to your younger students that in biblical times God's Word was written on an early form of paper made from plants. Since there were no books, these writings looked something like rolls of paper towels with sticks attached. These were called scrolls, and people rolled them out to read.

Take several sheets of 11 by 17 inch paper and cut them in half lengthwise (making them 5 1/2 by 17 inches). Help each student print a Bible verse on his piece of paper and tape the sheet to dowel rods. (If possible, paint the dowel rods gold ahead of time and tie a tassel at the top of each one.) Guide the children in rolling the paper into a scroll, then show them how to unroll it to read the Scripture to their parents and friends.

---

46 Make-It-Yourself Bible Picture Book

OBJECTIVE: To help children understand and express to others what the Bible says

Appropriate for ages 6 to 8

As an effective way to review Bible stories and reinforce Bible learning aims, prepare a creative drawing book for each of your students.

Staple together six to twelve sheets of white construction paper with colored sheets in front and back for a cover. Provide crayons and stickers for your students to decorate the front cover, making sure their names are included somewhere.

On each white page print a Scripture reference. Ask each class member to read the verse in his Bible and then draw a picture describing what the Scripture is about. Eventually his "book" will become his very own illustrated collection of Bible stories.

You may choose to tell the students to bring their books home to work on at their leisure or let the children draw when they are finished with other projects in class.

47 (Throw Out The Nets)

OBJECTIVE: To make the Bible come alive for younger children

Appropriate for ages 3 to 8

Young children tend to learn more by doing than by listening. To help your students understand Scripture, let them "play out" the Bible stories you tell. Here is one story to let your children play:

Set up the children's chairs to be their "boats." Scatter on the floor a dozen or so construction paper fish shapes cut from the pattern below. The children will put fish into an imaginary net in the center of the room (or perhaps you could obtain a fish net or make a "net" from a large piece of nylon net to add to the scene). Now the children are ready to "play" the story told in Luke 5:1-7:

Fishermen four went fishing one night;
Rowed in their boats with all of their might; (Row with large sideward strokes.)
Threw out their nets in the water—swish! (Throw out the nets.)
And drew them up, but found not a fish. (Draw up the nets and look carefully for a fish.)
They threw and pulled, threw and pulled some more, (Alternate throwing out and pulling in nets.)
'Til their shoulders and backs and arms were sore. (Rub sore shoulders and arms.)
When Jesus said, "Throw," they let down the net,

(Throw out the nets.)
Hoping at least a few fish to get.
This time the net took four men to pull! (Pull the net up part way.)
All the fish piled up till the boat was full! (Pick up fish shapes from floor and throw in the net.)

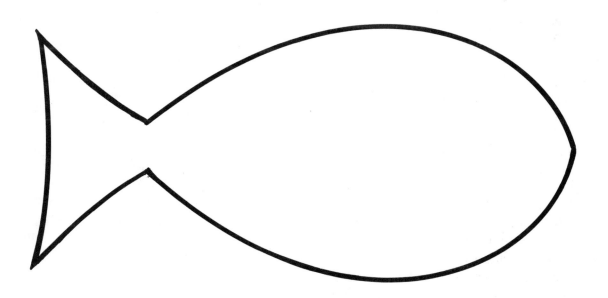

48 The Bible Is . . .

OBJECTIVE: To help children see an overall picture of what the Bible contains

Appropriate for ages 9 to 12

Prepare a bulletin board with a large cut-out shape of an open Bible and the words "The Bible is a Book of . . ." Cut envelopes in half (crosswise) to make pockets and secure these to the Bible shape. On each envelope pocket print one of these categories:

> Commands
> Stories
> Poems and Songs
> The Preaching of Prophets
> The Good News About Jesus
> Promises
> Teaching and Helping

Each week put in the various pockets slips of paper with questions (and Scripture references) that relate to the different categories. As your students arrive in the classroom, or during free activity time, they can select one of the questions and see if they can find the answer.

Some possible questions are:

Commands

1. In Joshua 1:9, what did the Lord say to Joshua as he was about to lead God's People to their new homeland? ("Have I not commanded thee? Be strong and of a good courage; be not afraid, neither be thou dismayed: for the Lord thy God is with thee whithersoever thou goest.")
2. What does Jesus say in Matthew 22:37 is the greatest commandment? ("Thou shalt love the Lord thy God with all thy heart, and with all thy soul, and with all thy mind.")
3. What does God want us to do, according to I John 3:23? ("This is His commandment, That we should believe on the Name of His Son Jesus Christ, and love one another, as He gave us commandment.")

Stories

1. What story will you read in Genesis 8? (How Noah and his family were kept safe during the flood)
2. What story is found in I Samuel 17 about a young boy who did a great and mighty act? (David and Goliath)
3. There is a story in Daniel 3 about three boys. What happened to them? (Shadrach, Meshach and Abednego were kept safe in the fiery

furnace by a fourth man, the Son of God.)

Poems and Songs

1. What does Psalm 118:14 say about the Lord? ("The Lord is my strength and song, and is become my salvation.")
2. What is the phrase that keeps repeating in Psalm 136? ("for His mercy endureth for ever")
3. What does Psalm 100:1-2 say we should do? ("Make a joyful noise unto the Lord, all ye lands. Serve the Lord with gladness; come before His presence with singing.")

The Preaching of Prophets

1. According to Isaiah 40:31, what will happen if we depend on the Lord when we feel weak? ("But they that wait upon the Lord shall renew their strength; they shall mount up with wings as eagles; they shall run, and not be weary; and they shall walk, and not faint.")
2. What does Micah 6:8 say the Lord requires of us? ("To do justly, and to love mercy, and to walk humbly with thy God.")
3. Malachi 3:10 says the Lord will open the windows of heaven and pour out a blessing, if we first do what? ("Bring all the tithes into the storehouse.")

The Good News About Jesus

1. What does Jesus say He came to do, according to Matthew 9:13? ("For I am not come to call

the righteous, but sinners to repentance.")

2. In Luke 2:49, what did Jesus tell his parents when they found Him in the temple at the age of twelve? ("How is it that ye sought Me? Wist not ye that I must be about My Father's business?")

3. What did Jesus tell Thomas in John 20:29? ("Thomas, because thou hast seen Me, thou hast believed: blessed are they that have not seen, and yet have believed.")

Promises

1. What does God promise us in II Corinthians 9:8? ("God is able to make all grace abound toward you; that ye, always having all sufficiency in all things, may abound to every good work.")

2. What does God promise in Romans 8:28? ("We know that all things work together for good to them that love God, to them who are called according to His purpose.")

3. What does the Lord promise us if we give, according to Luke 6:38? ("Give, and it shall be given unto you; good measure, pressed down, and shaken together, and running over, shall men give into your bosom. For with the same measure that ye mete withal it shall be measured to you again.")

Teaching and Helping

1. How should we talk, according to Ephesians 4:29? ("Let no corrupt communication proceed out of your mouth, but that which is good to

the use of edifying, that it may minister grace unto the hearers.")

2. According to II Timothy 3:16, why is Scripture given to us? ("All Scripture is given by inspiration of God, and is profitable for doctrine, for reproof, for correction, for instruction in righteousness.")

3. What does III John 11 say we should follow? ("Beloved, follow not that which is evil, but that which is good. He that doeth good is of God: but he that doeth evil hath not seen God.")

49 Bible Story Password

OBJECTIVE: To reinforce Bible lessons through an easy game format

Appropriate for ages 6 to 12

With the children in your class sitting down and facing the front of the room, divide the class into two teams. Send one person from each team to the back of the room and have the players face the back wall. Write a word on a slip of paper — the name of a Bible character or place, or a Bible story — for the rest of the children to see, then put it away.

Tell the children at the back of the room to come forward and take turns trying to guess the answer. The first team will give a one-word clue relating to the name or story. For instance, if the answer is Joseph, the team can say "coat" or "dreams," etc. Give the player a chance to think of an answer. If he is not correct, play goes to the other team, and so on back and forth until one child finally gets it right. Then two more children go to the back of the room and wait for the next word. The first team to get 10 points wins.

50 Help The Scribes

OBJECTIVE: To encourage children to learn Scriptures correctly

Appropriate for ages 8 to 12

Duplicate the puzzle on page 61 for each student to have a copy. Explain to the class that the "scribes" have been copying Scriptures onto the scrolls, but they have made some mistakes. Instruct the children to look up the verses in their Bibles to find the incorrect words and replace them with the correct ones.

After the students finish the puzzle, help them memorize one or two of the verses. One easy method is to write a verse on the chalkboard or dry erase board. Say the verse together several times, then erase a few words and say it again. Repeat this process until you have erased the entire verse, then ask if anyone would like to say the verse by himself.

Answers are on page 64.

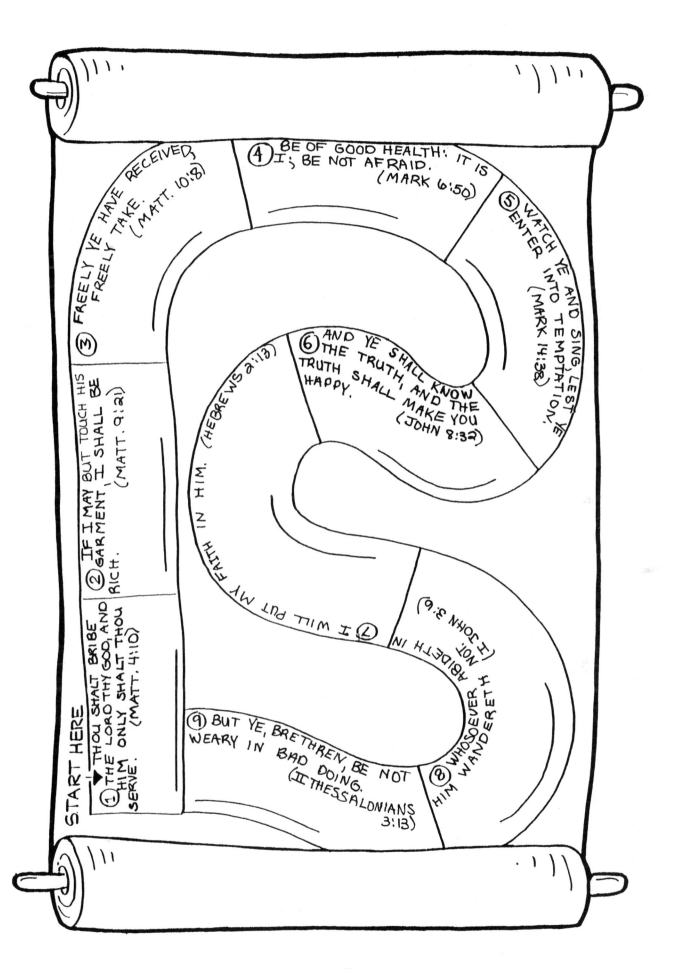

START HERE

① THOU SHALT BRIBE THE LORD THY GOD, AND HIM ONLY SHALT THOU SERVE. (MATT. 4:10)

② IF I MAY BUT TOUCH HIS GARMENT, I SHALL BE RICH. (MATT. 9:21)

③ FREELY YE HAVE RECEIVED, FREELY TAKE. (MATT. 10:8)

④ BE OF GOOD HEALTH: IT IS I; BE NOT AFRAID. (MARK 6:50)

⑤ WATCH YE AND SING, LEST YE ENTER INTO TEMPTATION. (MARK 14:38)

⑥ AND YE SHALL KNOW THE TRUTH, AND THE TRUTH SHALL MAKE YOU HAPPY. (JOHN 8:32)

⑦ I WILL PUT MY FAITH IN HIM. (HEBREWS 2:13)

⑧ WHOSOEVER ABIDETH IN HIM WANDERETH NOT. (I JOHN 3:6)

⑨ BUT YE, BRETHREN, BE NOT WEARY IN BAD DOING. (II THESSALONIANS 3:13)

51 The Bible Says God Loves Us

OBJECTIVE: To provide opportunity for children to accept the Lord as their personal Savior

Appropriate for all ages

Jesus said, "Suffer the little children to come unto Me" (Mark 10:14). Our main objective in Christian education is to introduce children to the Lord Jesus Christ and to help them come to know Him as their Savior and Lord.

Evangelism is a threefold process, which has sometimes been likened to the planting of a seed. First, the soil must be cultivated and prepared; second, the seed which has been planted sprouts and produces life; third, the plant grows to maturity.

Similarly, the goal of Christian education is threefold: First, to prepare hearts for a decision for Christ; second, to lead the child to accept Christ as Savior; third, to build the child up in Christ and help him grow to Christian maturity.

It is important to recognize that there is no set time at which a child is ready to accept Christ as Savior. Often those who have received Christian training in their homes and at Sunday school and church are ready to make this decision at an earlier age than other children.

Only the Holy Spirit knows the time at which a child is spiritually prepared to accept Christ as Savior, and only He can perform the miracle of the new birth. We can "plant" and "water," but only the Holy Spirit can produce results.

Remember that one characteristic of young children is that they desire to please adult leaders. They are also "copy cats" and will do whatever their best friends do. For this reason it is important to be cautious in giving group invitations. You may choose to explain the plan of salvation carefully to the entire class, but set aside time to talk individually with any student who expresses a desire to ask Jesus to be his Savior. Let the child express himself and be careful not to put words in his mouth. And most importantly, pray for the guidance of the Holy Spirit.

Use your Bible frequently as you present the plan of salvation to your class:

a. Read I John 4:19 to show the children that God loves us very much.

b. Point out that we have all done wrong. As it

says in Romans 3:23, the Bible calls wrongdoing sin, and sin separates us from the love of God. According to Romans 6:23, sin must be punished.

c. God loves us so much that He sent His own perfect Son to take the punishment for our sins. Read I Corinthians 15:3 and Romans 5:8 to emphasize this point.

d. Explain that although God's gift of life is free, it doesn't come to us automatically. We must be truly sorry for our sins and ask Jesus to be our Savior. John 1:12 and 3:16 tell us we need to believe that God's Son died for us, and I John 1:9 tells us what God will do when we express that belief and say we are sorry for our sin.

When meeting with the students individually, ask each one if he would like to kneel and pray with you. Help the child to ask Jesus to be his Savior and to forgive him for his sins. Assure him that God has forgiven his sins and that he is now a member of God's family. Encourage him to tell others of his decision, and be sure to talk with his parents about the step he has taken and how they can help him in his walk with Jesus.

52 Bible Newscasters

OBJECTIVE: To create interest in studying the Bible and help children learn its meaning

Appropriate for age 10 to teens (and the entire congregation)

Turn your students into television newscasters as a novel way to get them to dig into the Bible to see what it actually says. Divide the class into various news teams: weather, world events, national scene, sports, science, etc. Then assign a Bible passage to each team and tell its members to write their own newscast according to what they find in the text. You might be amazed with what some groups come up with (and how thoroughly they will search the Scriptures.)

Give each news team plenty of time to read the assigned passages and write its copy for the telecast. It would be best to not try to squeeze this kind of teaching method into a few minutes; provide at least an hour or more for your students to study the Bible and write the news copy.

You can use this approach with many kinds of Bible passages. For example, in the Old Testament, Judges 6 and 7 provide opportunity for a "war correspondent" report as well as commentary by a "national affairs analyst." Or you might suggest someone play the part of Gideon and have a "panel of experts" interview him in a sort of "Meet the Press" encounter.

Another idea is to use Romans 12 and report it as a speech given by an internationally known diplomat (Paul, who is known as Christ's ambassador). Your students could interpret Paul's ideas in light of what could happen socially, or what might happen with the money system, or how the form of government could change. In the latter portions of Romans 12, the children could interview a "guest psychologist" on the harmful effects of seeking revenge against neighbors, fellow workers or family members for real or imagined offenses they have committed.

If your class is studying the Book of Acts, the newscast approach has many possibilities. The first eight or nine chapters of Acts provide all kinds of material for "on the spot" reporting.

At the end of the class session, the teams should have most if not all of their newscasts written. The following week, bring a "television"

for the students to make their presentations. (Ahead of time, cut out two parallel sides of a large box and draw a control panel with numbers for the channels and buttons for on/off and volume.) If your church stores Bible-times costumes such as for Christmas presentations, see if your class members can borrow some outfits. The children will enjoy dressing up and the costumes will lend authenticity to the project.

Ask the students to listen attentively to each other during the newscast, then allow time for discussion of the biblical events. Try to get the children to think about how the stories relate to us today.

You may want to ask the pastor for a time slot when the children could present their newscasts to the rest of the congregation. The children and adults alike will appreciate the chance to express creativity in Bible learning.

Another idea:

Instead of using a cardboard television, videotape the student's newscasts. This will make the project even more realistic and enjoyable for them and for the congregation.

Answer Page

Bible Words Puzzle
page 13

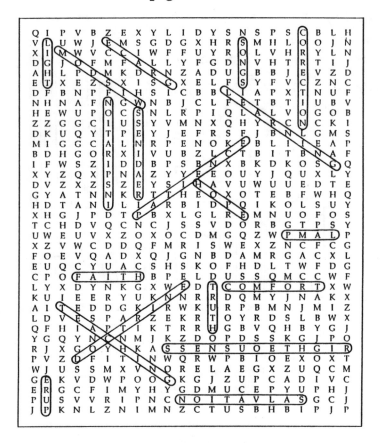

Books Within A Book Crossword
page 23

Parent-Child Proverbs
page 25

a. a garland to grace your head and a chain to adorn your neck
b. grief to his mother
c. heeds his father's instruction
d. is careful to discipline him
e. gains understanding
f. you will be wise
g. he will not turn from it
h. is wise
i. keep to my ways
j. a discerning son
k. who destroys

Meet The Writer Matching Quiz
page 31

1. f   5. d
2. a   6. c
3. e   7. b
4. h   8. g

Paul's Letters Puzzle
page 37

a. Philippians   g. Philemon
b. II Corinthians h. I Timothy
c. Titus   i. I Corinthians
d. Galatians   j. II Thessalonians
e. Ephesians   k. Romans
f. I Thessalonians l. Colossians

Help The Scribes
page 61

1. bribe/worship
2. rich/whole
3. take/give
4. health/cheer
5. sing/pray
6. happy/free
7. faith/trust
8. wandereth/sinneth
9. bad/well